GLASGOW AND DUNBARTONSHIRE INDEPENDENTS

David Devoy

AMBERLEY

First published 2017

Amberley Publishing
The Hill, Stroud
Gloucestershire, GL5 4EP

www.amberley-books.com

Copyright © David Devoy, 2017

The right of David Devoy to be identified as
the Author of this work has been asserted in
accordance with the Copyrights, Designs and
Patents Act 1988.

ISBN 978 1 4456 7446 9 (print)
ISBN 978 1 4456 7447 6 (ebook)

British Library Cataloguing in Publication Data.
A catalogue record for this book is available from
the British Library.

Origination by Amberley Publishing.
Printed in the UK.

Setting the Scene

Glasgow is the largest city in Scotland, and third largest in the United Kingdom. Historically part of Lanarkshire, it is now one of the thirty-two council areas of Scotland and is situated on the River Clyde in the country's west central Lowlands. Inhabitants of the city are referred to as Glaswegians. The city grew from a small rural settlement on the River Clyde to become the largest seaport in Britain, and the University was established in the fifteenth century. From the eighteenth century the city also grew as one of Great Britain's main hubs of transatlantic trade with North America and the West Indies. With the onset of the Industrial Revolution, the population and economy of Glasgow and the surrounding region expanded rapidly to become one of the world's pre-eminent centres of chemicals, textiles and engineering; most notably in the shipbuilding and marine engineering industry, which produced many innovative and famous vessels. Glasgow was the 'Second City of the British Empire' for much of the Victorian era and Edwardian period, although many cities argue the title was theirs.

In the late nineteenth and early twentieth centuries Glasgow grew in population, reaching a peak of 1,128,473 in 1939. Comprehensive urban renewal projects in the 1960s, resulting in large-scale relocation of people to new towns and peripheral suburbs, followed by successive boundary changes, reduced the population of the City of Glasgow council area to 599,650 with 1,209,143 people living in the Greater Glasgow urban area. The entire region surrounding the conurbation covers about 2.3 million people, 41 per cent of Scotland's population. At the 2011 census, Glasgow had a population density that was the highest of any Scottish city.

Local bus and tram services were traditionally operated by the Corporation Transport Department, which had a monopoly in the city limits from 1930 onwards. This meant buses of the Scottish Bus Group and others could not pick up passengers once they passed the city boundary, although passengers could be set down. As the city expanded this only covered the boundaries up to 1938, meaning that any development built after this had to be shared with buses of the Scottish Bus Group. A couple of independents worked into the city. Lowland Motorways had a network of routes in the east end but sold out to the Bus Group in the 1950s, leaving Paton's of Renfrew to reach the suburb of Govan, worked from Paisley via Renfrew from 1958. They were joined in 1963 when Graham's of Paisley were granted a licence linking Govan with Linwood via Penilee. Smith's of Barrhead served the South Nitshill housing scheme from Paisley until selling out to Western SMT in 1968. In 1980 McGill's of Barrhead introduced a new service linking Auchenback to Glasgow city centre after a court battle with Strathclyde PTE, which had taken over from the corporation.

The neighbouring county of Dumbarton adjoins the city and is bordered by the River Clyde, and extends as far as Cumbernauld to the east. Bus companies in the area running services included Highland of Glenboig, who sold out to Alexander Midland in 1968, Garelochhead Coach Services, who went into administration in 1980, and Barrie's of Balloch.

Everything changed, however, when local bus services in the UK were de-regulated in 1986. This effectively allowed any credible operator to register and run a local bus service. Many companies decided to wait a while to see what would happen before committing resources. Hutchison's of Overtown began an hourly service from Coltness via Wishaw and were soon joined by Barrie's of Balloch. Barrie's had been a coach operator with a modern fleet that was renewed every couple of years. They relied heavily on MOD contracts, which were lost, causing the fleet to be greatly reduced. Eight ex-Green Line Leopards were purchased to work a new network of services registered in the Vale of Leven. The network expanded the following year, but in February 1988 the entire fleet was grounded after maintenance problems. A fleet of hired buses was used until the company ceased trading on 25 April. Allander Travel of Milngavie wanted to purchase the business, but it was heavily in debt, so they reactivated a dormant subsidiary named County Coaches (PSV Scotland) Ltd. This was renamed as Loch Lomond Coaches Ltd and continued to run from Barrie's depot in Alexandria, using a similar livery of red and cream. Barrie's had only moved to the former torpedo factory in 1987. John Morrow Coaches had registered some school journeys and linked them to run as service 86 in the Clydebank, Duntocher and Old Kilpatrick areas. In Kirkintilloch, Ann's Coaches registered a local service from February 1987.

Elsewhere in the region many commuter journeys operated by independents reached the city, mainly at peak hours. Services not registered commercially were put out to tender. Early examples of this were Henderson Travel with the Shawlands to Muirend and Pollok to Kennishead routes. A remarkable tender was announced in November 1987 when Wilson's of Carnwath obtained the Glasgow inter-station service 98. A seemingly unrelated event around this time concerned a coach and school contracts company named Duncan Stewart Coaches, based at Dalmuir. The firm had been established in the 1960s and had ironically taken some of the MOD work previously run by Barrie's. The death of the founder saw the business turned into a co-operative of former staff with Jack Hinde, Liam McColl, John Boyce and Ian MacTavish taking over the day-to-day running.

August 1987 saw John Morrow register route 86 as an all-day service, while two months later Castle Coaches of Alexandria registered two commercial routes. The new Balloch to Alexandria and Bonhill to Tillichewan services were operated by Barrie's, but had been given up due to ongoing maintenance problems. Two Ford service buses were obtained for this work. Green's of Kirkintilloch were another coach operator with ambitions. Their depot was the old railway goods yard in Kirkintilloch, but this was needed for a new road development and was subject to a compulsory purchase order. A new site in the town was purchased from Wimpy the builders and comprised of factory units and a large hard-standing area. Most of the units were rented out, but a new paint shop and maintenance unit were established. Major operator Kelvin Scottish was distraught when new services were registered from 23 December 1987. Routes to Glasgow from Campsie Glen and Harestanes via Kirkintilloch began. This was competition on a larger scale than hitherto.

February 1988 saw Whitelaw's of Stonehouse obtain the tender for a Milton to Anniesland route, surprising everyone as their base was over twenty miles away. Ann's Coaches registered a second route from Kirkintilloch to Waterside, and Henderson Travel started running commercially on the Mount Vernon to Rutherglen service. A new face joined the fray when Crainey of Kilsyth won the tender for a Cumbernauld to Kilsyth route. With operators starting and ending services at a seemingly relentless pace, it looked as if the industry lacked stability. Former Midland driver John Morrow realised this early on and decided to re-use old service numbers that had been discarded by the larger operators. He re-used the former numbers used by Central SMT in the Clydebank area. In April 1989 he expanded his route network in the area with a Clydebank to Duntocher circular, Linnvale to Faifley and Whitecrook to Drumchapel routes. Four ex-Midland Leopards were obtained in March 1989 to run this extra work. Fleet numbers were introduced at this time, and a new depot at Barclay Curle Estate was obtained to house the expanding fleet. Crainey obtained more vehicles to match the frequency operated by Kelvin Scottish between Cumbernauld and Kilsyth, while Canavan of Croy began a peak-hour Glasgow to Harestanes route in August, also adding a Cumbernauld town centre to Condorrat service. Dunn's of Airdrie also launched a peak-hour Glasgow to Cumbernauld service. On 2 August the Glasgow station service passed from Wilson's to John Morrow, with Leyland Nationals being obtained to run it. Green's continued to expand and a ten-minute frequency was being run on the combined Glasgow to Kirkintilloch routes. September saw John Morrow add six new routes to his network. Crainey tried a Kilsyth to Glasgow peak-hour service from late 1989, but it was withdrawn in April the following year. Allander Travel launched a further two services in the Dumbarton area.

1990 came and McKenna's of Uddingston began running services 234/6 from the city to Uddingston. Castle Coaches bowed out in February, but former Duncan Stewart partner Liam McColl began a Clydebank to Haldane route, running hourly. One of the last traditional independents folded on 27 April when Graham's of Paisley ceased all services. This left McGill's of Barrhead to fly the flag alone and they moved the terminal for their Glasgow to Auchenback service from Montrose Street into Buchanan bus station. Pringle of Bearsden began operating Glasgow tours in April 1990 and this would flourish as the years passed. Canavan began an Abronhill to Cumbernauld local service and Green's formed a separate company to buy and sell vehicles. They formed Regal Coach Sales and were bidding for large batches of second-hand vehicles. Some would enter their own fleet while others would be resold to other operators. A very surprising development saw a joint network with Kelvin Central Buses registered. Loch Lomond Coaches Ltd ceased trading in March 1991, but all services and vehicles were transferred to the parent Allander Travel fleet. Four months later a joint service network with Kelvin Central Buses was also announced. Kelvin Central was in the throes of privatisation at the time and this seemed like the precursor to a take-over. August 1991 saw the formation of Avondale Coaches in Greenock by Thomas MacIntyre, and this firm would later feature in the story. In the south of the city two ex-Clydeside Scottish drivers named McKie and Young set up the Govan Minibus Company to operate around the Govan area. To finish off the year Dunn's of Airdrie launched a Cumbernauld local service, while McKenna's launched a Glasgow to Motherwell service from 3 October. Beaton's of Blantyre began a Hamilton to Glasgow service, but it would not last long. 1 December saw Green's sell their service network to Kelvin Central Buses, with many vehicles changing hands plus an agreement with Regal Coach sales to provide more.

1992 kicked off with Allander Travel sharing the KCB depot at Old Kilpatrick, although heavy overhauls were sent to the company's Milngavie depot. January also saw services registered by Folley of Clydebank, linking Clydebank, Partick, Maryhill, Dalmuir and Summerston. A night service was also introduced from Glasgow to Clydebank at weekends. The introduction of an hourly Glasgow to Erskine service operated by Bridge Coaches of Erskine began on 10 February, and increased to every fifteen minutes from 13 April. March saw KCB take over McKenna's of Uddingston as the owner wished to retire. Canavan re-registered the former Green's service linking Glasgow and Kirkintilloch on a twenty-minute headway, but this was increased to every fifteen minutes from June when the route was jointly worked with Crainey's of Kilsyth. Stewart Dickson began operating service 38, linking the city with Paisley Cross via Paisley Road West. John Morrow upped the competition with KCB, adding new services and double-deck buses for the first time. 13 July saw the introduction of a forty-minute frequency service by Hutchison's of Renfrew, which followed that of Dickson's. Lianne's of Renfrew tried a Renfrew to Mosspark service briefly. The commercial services of McColl's and PJ Travel of Dalmuir passed to KCB from August. From 4 September Bellview Coaches of Paisley began a Glasgow to Paisley Cross service using AEC Routemasters, but it would not last long. The same day witnessed another new operator hit the road when Puma Coaches began with a Govan to Pollok service. Weir's Tours of Clydebank began operating services in the Garelochhead area. On 19 September John Morrow sold his services to KCB along with thirty-one vehicles, but would remain in business as a coach operator.

Bellview quit their Glasgow service in January 1993, while Folley registered two ex-John Morrow services abandoned by KCB in the Old Kilpatrick and Duntocher areas. Crainey came to an arrangement with KCB the following month, when the city was abandoned in favour of local services worked jointly around Cumbernauld. KCB lost the Glasgow station service acquired from Morrow to HAD Coaches of Shotts. Strathclyde Buses launched their low-cost subsidiary in August to combat the ever-growing competition. Canavan's also quit the city in favour of services around Cumbernauld after an agreement with KCB in March. Alexandria Coaches registered the Luss to Alexandria service given up by Allander/KCB. April saw Hutchison's of Renfrew increase their Paisley to Govan route to run every twelve minutes, while Puma started a second route around Pollok. Red Lion of Uddingston ran a Glasgow to Motherwell service from May until December before giving up, while Ross Coaches tried a Mosspark to Renfrew Street peak-hour service for about four months. Rounding the year off, Folley added Clydebank to Bonhill and St Enoch to Duntocher services and Goldline of Paisley ran a Cardonald to city service from 15 December until February 1994.

Donald Bagley of Alexandria, t/a DEB Travel, launched an Eaglesham to city service from February 1994 until pulling the plug in August due to heavy duplication by GCT. The following month saw Castle Coaches cease trading, while Folley was called to a Traffic Commissioners' inquiry, resulting in all services being cancelled. May saw Govan Minibus Co. launch a Govan to Penilee route, while McColl's purchased the former Barrie's depot in Balloch. Red Lion of Uddingston extended their Motherwell service into the city from 3 May but cancelled it from 24 September. Green Line of Paisley registered the former Clydeside 2000 service 16 from South Nitshill to Glasgow in June, but had given up by 25 July. Munro of Uddingston ran into the city from Hamilton from the start of the year, but withdrew in June after agreement with KCB. Puma extended their original route into the city centre in September, but not for long. Blue Line of Johnstone tried a Penilee to Pollok service briefly before moving elsewhere. A significant event for all operators occurred when Strathclyde Buses gained control of KCB, who purchased the remaining part of Green's business in November.

1995 began with two new companies challenging Weir's in the Helensburgh/ Coulport area when McQueen of Garelochhead and Wilson's of Rhu combined their forces. Weir's gave up all interests in the area from 10 November. Another new operator appeared when Riverside Transport registered the former Clydeside route 16 from South Nitshill to the city. McColl's won the Luss to Alexandria service on retendering in July. Greenock-based Ashton Coaches reached the city in July when their Largs route was extended to Partick. Goldline Travel re-emerged on 2 November with a city to Penilee route, while from 6 December Walker of Dalmuir commenced working from Clydebank to Drumchapel. This lasted until 6 October 1997.

On 11 May 1996 Allander Travel sold their bus services to SB Holdings, partly because the garage at Old Kilpatrick was being closed. Ashton registered a new route linking Port Glasgow to the city from April and a Nethercraigs route was also added. McColl's added Dumbarton and Helensburgh locals from 26 April. Ashton subsidiary Coastline Express began a Glasgow to Bishopton service as well as re-registering some of the Ashton routes in their own name. Dart Buses of Paisley was formed by ex-Clydeside staff with thirty buses and registered a Glasgow to Bridge of Weir route, while David Bishop, t/a DB Travel, launched a Clydebank to Faifley service in September. A familiar face re-appeared from 21 October when John Morrow began a Linnvale to Parkhall service. Major operator SB Holdings became part of Firstbus.

Bellview Coaches of Paisley started a Clydebank to city service in early 1997, but had their licences revoked in June. Govan Minibus Company went into receivership, but was replaced by a new company named First Stop Travel, financed by the former owner of DEB Travel and based in Kilmaurs. The Cowie Group had purchased Clydeside 2000 and added Ashton Coaches Group with sixty-two vehicles to their portfolio, as well as 25 per cent of Dart Buses. Phil Doherty, t/a PD Travel, began operating from Clydebank to Mountblow, but this was quickly changed to Faifley. Riverside added a Paisley to Nitshill service from 8 June, while Lochview Coaches won the Clydebank to Glasgow Airport tender. John Boyce began a Glasgow to Kirkintilloch route every two hours. S&A Coaches was formed by Stewart Dickson and Allan Arnott, but the service between the city and Eastwood Toll ran as City Sprinter from December 1997.

Carlton Coaches began the year with a Clydebank to Dalmuir service, but withdrew it on 20 April, only to try a service to Glasgow from 22 June. PD Travel began a Drumchapel to Clydebank service in March, followed by a Dalmuir to city, and Faifley to Partick network. DB Travel followed in April with a Glasgow/Duntocher/ Faifley service. Meanwhile, Coakley of Motherwell reached the city from Hamilton. Dart Buses won the tender for an Anniesland to Ruchill service in July. An event that would later influence matters was the award of the Clydebank/Dumbarton dial-a-bus to Avondale Coaches of Greenock. First Stop Travel began expanding and added a Govan to Croftfoot route.

1999 witnessed the take-over of Hutchison's of Renfrew by Arriva. Carlton had changed routes four times in eighteen months, while Coakley added more routes into the city when a service to Airdrie commenced. First Stop added Govan to Castlemilk and Govan to South Nitshill routes in November. John Morrow launched a Dalmuir/ Duntocher circular, and Weir's tried a Clydebank to Braehead Shopping Centre route, which ran from October 1999 until April 2000. November saw Gleniffer Coaches adopt the Govan to Paisley service, served by Hutchison's until Arriva took over. Former Firstbus manager Russell Arden started Glasgow Citybus with a Glasgow to Duntocher route. Skyline Travel, which was associated with Puma Coaches, tried a Braehead to Pollok route between 22 November 1999 and April 2000. PD travel tried other services, including city to Balornock East and Clydebank to Drumchapel.

The new century saw McColl's register a Balloch to Dumbarton service, commencing 2 February. New operator Scotway Travel, which was associated with Bellview, began a Glagow to Barrhead service from 11 January, and was joined by the associated Local Bus Company of Greenock from 10 July with a Glasgow to Paisley route. On 3 July PD Travel cancelled most routes in order to concentrate its resources on the Faifley to Partick Corridor, and in August all licences were transferred to Bayview Enterprises, based in Helensburgh. Avondale Coaches of Greenock opened a fourteen-bus subsidiary based in Dock Street in Clydebank, in premises once used by Weirs, Morrow and PD Travel. Three routes were registered: Linnvale to Drumchapel, Faifley to Knightwood and Glasgow. Meanwhile, on 20 November Glasgow Citybus launched a Glasgow to Cadder route.

2001 kicked off when Gibson's of Renfrew added a Glasgow to Erskine service, while McKindless of Wishaw entered the city from Wishaw a week later. Avondale cancelled the Linnvale route in favour of a Clydebank to Duntocher service on 28 February. Not to be outdone, City Sprinter opened a second front with a Clarkston Toll to city route, but abandoned it in July after heavy competition. Stagecoach Glasgow franchised their X8/9/10 routes to Dart Buses and purchased the Arriva shareholding in the firm in April. On 28 May Avondale added a Drumchapel to Radnor Street and Drumchapel circular, while PD Travel's owner added a second company, which traded as Beta Buses from 5 June. Scotway launched a city to airport facility at the end of May. Coakley of Motherwell had all licences revoked, but a solution was found when William Nelson registered all the routes and hired buses from Coakley to operate them. Sadly, Dart Buses crashed overnight on 26 October, and allegedly punished Stagecoach for not helping them by giving First Glasgow time to register all the routes before the end.

A new operator began on 3 January 2002, when the Caledonian Coach Company of Kilmarnock was formed. However, they quickly registered services in Glasgow, running to Castlemilk and East Kilbride. PD Travel tried a city to Milton route and Jim Geary resurrected the Linwood Clipper service once operated by Graham's of Paisley, even using the same livery. McKindless staked new territory from 22 January when they began running to Kirkintilloch. Avondale had been a partnership between Messrs McIntyre and Irving, but it was dissolved and the Greenock operations were split off and merged with Slaemuir Coaches. Irving maintained the Avondale name and Clydebank operations. Puma owner Tony Morrin started another business and Colchri Coaches won the tenders for the Pollok to Shawlands and Milngavie to Kirkintilloch services. Perhaps the most significant event occurred when McGill's of Port Glasgow was formed on 15 April. As the years went by, they would creep ever nearer to the city. On 8 May Scotway had its licences revoked and three days later Firstbus launched a competitive route against Canavan in Cumbernauld, only to find the independent retaliate with a city to Garthamlock service.

2003 started off quietly and it wasn't until June that Morrow began operating from Clydebank to Mountblow. September witnessed a joint network begin when Avondale and McColl's began service 215, linking Clydebank and Balloch. McColl's also ran service 204, linking both places by a different route. PJ Travel ran from Clydebank to Helensburgh, while John Boyce added a similar route from October. On 15 October Caledonian began two more routes: St Enoch to Carmunock and Charing Cross to Newton Mearns, while PD Travel began a Partick to Gartnavel Hospital service in December.

2004 saw a lot of cancellations, from PD Travel, Morrow and Canavan, but Avondale extended their Drumchapel service into the city. Coakley continued their fight with the Traffic Commisioners, with appeals and counter-appeals. Eventually the Nelson licence was surrendered and services resumed under the Coakley name. Alan Thomson registered a second company when Linn Park Buses began with a Cathkin to Auchinairn route. First Stop Travel moved to a new depot near Renfrew Ferry, and John Morrow began a second company. The Clydebank Bus Company began a Blairdardie to Anniesland route on 24 August. Gibson's sold their interest in the Paisley to Govan service to First Stop Travel in October, along with seven vehicles, while A&P Coaches began new services linking Pollok to Carnwadric and Mosspark to Braehead Shopping Centre. Another new company was formed when McColl's set up Loch Lomond Bus Services Ltd, based at Renton. Linn Park started running from East Kilbride to Clydebank from 28 September, while DB Travel began operating from Dalmuir to Glasgow on 15 November.

Caledonian started a Castlemilk to city service from 11 January, and set up a third company, trading as New Concept Coaches, to operate between the city and Glasgow Airport. This would run until November 2006. Avondale withdrew their Clydebank to Braehead Shopping Centre route after only six months. First Glasgow abandoned the ex-Dart Buses service linking the city to Kilmacolm, but this was taken over by Slaemuir Coaches and some journeys were extended to Greenock. Morrow launched a Charing Cross to Drumchapel service, but it didn't last long. In November the Canavan family found their services in Cumbernauld under attack by Peter Canavan after a family dispute. First Stop Travel ownership passed to Slaemuir Coaches, but they sold the Govan to Paisley route on to Arriva.

2006 began with West Coast Motors purchasing the Glasgow Citybus business, and Dunn of Cumbernauld started an express service X3 into the city. Gibson's of Renfrew re-registered the Govan to Paisley service sold to First Stop, and Puma and Colchri moved to new premises at the Westway Development in Renfrew. PJ Travel services ended abruptly in February after a depot fire destroyed eleven vehicles, Weir's of Clydebank closed down and Avondale quit their share of the Clydebank to Balloch service. First Stop Travel changed hands once again after John Walker acquired it, and Gullivers Travel, another Walker Group company, tried a Glasgow circular briefly. Skyline tried Pollok to Govan and Pollok local routes, and Colchri launched service 22 linking Pollok and Braehead Shopping Centre. McGill's finally reached the city from 23 October when a Largs to Glasgow route was initiated. The year finished when Caledonian launched Nethercraigs and Kennishead routes to the city. Negotiations for a take-over between First Stop Travel and Dickson's broke down.

First Stop launched a competing service against Dickson's on the Paisley Road West corridor, and Dickson's responded with posters on their buses informing the public that they didn't run un-named buses. The Walker Group then ran look-alike buses from 21 February in white with the fleet name Dickson's of Erskine Limited. McKindless began running from Faifley to Glasgow and Morrow introduced a Bishopbriggs circular. McColl's moved to a new depot in Alexandria. Hutchison's of Overtown sold out to Firstbus in July, and McGill's began services linking the city to Helensburgh and Balloch. The Walker Group set up another new company when

Flying Scotsman (Roadtrain Ltd) was registered. McColl's gave up the Clydebank to Balloch service, but John Boyce registered it instead. Fairline Coaches began a city to airport service from 24 July, and City Sprinter tried a 38A service serving Woodfarm. The Walker Group started to target other independents and registered a Neilston to Braehead service against A&P Coaches, and a Paisley to Hawkhead and Paisley to Bridge of Weir route against Riverside. Riverside retaliated with a Govan to Drumoyne route. Slaemuir Coaches passed their X7 Kilmacolm to Glasgow service to McGill's.

February 2008 saw Peter Canavan sell out to Coakley of Motherwell, while the Barrhead Bus Company launched a Paisley to Braehead route on 15 March. Neil Stafford began a Paisley to Glasgow service in the evenings at the weekends from 9 May, while August witnessed McGill's start a Glasgow to Dunoon route. The Walker Group had all its licences revoked from 15 August, and Barrhead depot had passed to Greenock & Distict Omnibuses the day before. G&D traded under the fleetname of United and all the ex-FST Govan-based services were registered. The company used the same livery as their parent, McGill's of Greenock. Further casualties between July and November saw PD Travel/Beta Buses and DB Travel all cease operations. McColl's re-registered all their services in the name of Loch Lomond Bus Services from 22 September, while October brought Linn Park Buses' demise. The associated New Concept Coaches registered a Castlemilk to Glasgow route, but by 27 October all Thomson Group services had ceased. A&P Coaches also closed down in the same month. In November 2008 Astrascreen of Paisley applied for the ex-FST services based around Govan and new routes between Castlemilk and Parkhead Forge/city centre. The firm was set up by George Findlay and originally traded as Comet Coaches, later selling out to Slaemuir Coaches. When Slaemuir sold their services in Inverclyde the company passed to McGill's. They, however, re-sold it immediately to Graeme Henderson. The Traffic Commissioners alleged that the business was being used as a front for another company, but this was refuted. The company did however operate from the ex-Walker Group Paisley depot and used many ex-Walker Group vehicles, before the licences were all revoked.

2009 witnessed MacKenzie of Cumbernauld start a Twechar to Cumbernauld route, Avondale began a Dumbarton to Clydebank route in May and United established new links between Neilston/Braehead and Silverburn. McColl's appeared on the Balloch to Westfield corridor from 20 June, later adding a Glasgow to Dumbarton facility. McGill's and their United subsidiary launched a new route from Glasgow to Erskine, although the United identity was dropped after 21 September.

The McKindless Group collapsed overnight on 19 February 2010, and Lippen Coaches ceased operations in April. The same month, however, saw Glasgow Citybus start a new route linking Clydebank to Faifley. A new operator, Coach & Commercial (UK) Ltd, t/a Kip Coaches, began operating between Braehead and Easterhouse but had given up by 12 August, and used the former Walker Group Paisley depot. Was this another front for someone? McGill's expanded once again when the services of Gibson's of Renfrew were acquired on 8 November. Meanwhile, Puma Coaches merged with Colchri on 1 September.

2011 saw Skyline launch a city to Battlefield route from 25 March, and Coakley ceased operations on 18 April. Meanwhile, McGill's purchased Dickson's in May and Colchri registered a new Govan to Paisley route. Wilson's of Gourock suffered an arson attack on their depot in June, and 20 August would see McColl's cancel most of their Dumbarton services. Skyline ceased operations on 3 August; director Francis Dolan had also been a director of Colchri up until 2009. MacKenzie Travel passed to Coakley, but still ran under their original name. In September control of City Sprinter passed to Enfield Coaches, based in Ireland.

On 26 March 2012 McGill's doubled their fleet by purchasing the Scottish operations of Arriva. The deal was referred to the Competition Commission, but later cleared. McColl's withdrew all their services that served Glasgow on 30 March. John Morrow retired from the industry and sold his services to Glasgow Citybus from 31 March. Law Bus & Coach went into receivership on 4 August and Stuart's of Carluke took over the Glasgow to Lanark express. Ann McKay set up a new Skyline company and registered a Govan to Silverburn service from 3 September, followed by a Govan local in November. Loch Lomond Bus Services sold their depot and thirty buses to McGill's in December, and McGill's registered a new Glasgow to Balloch Express from that time.

City Sprinter launched a service linking Castlemilk to the city on 6 May 2013, and ran it until August 2014. Glasgow Citybus registered a Milngavie to Glasgow route. Meanwhile, Avondale moved to a new depot in Dock Street in Clydebank, and City Sprinter adopted new premises in Nitshill. McGill's decided to close their Dumbarton depot from 3 November and all commercial services in the area were cancelled. The following year saw Avondale start a Clydebank local, while Colchri registered a Pollok to Nitshill route.

2015 began when McNairn's registered the city to Stobhill Hospital service commercially. Colchri began a Pollok to Nitshill route on 4 May, and Glasgow Citybus de-registered their Old Kilpatrick to Gartnavel Hospital service. City Sprinter ceased its services abruptly on 2 July, after a police inquiry was launched at the behest of the Traffic Commisioners. Skyline ceased all services from 28 July, while Colchri added a Silverburn to Queen Elizabeth Hospital route. Glasgow Citybus won the tendered inter-station service in August, and McGill's stepped in to cover some of the former Skyline services. McGill's also started to run the Fastlink service F1, linking the new Queen Elizabeth Hospital to the city via a dedicated busway.

In January 2016 West Coast Motors' owners, Craig's of Campbeltown, increased their vehicle allowance to 255 to absorb all their subsidiary companies. On 4 April McGill's took over McNairn's, adding the Stobhill Hospital service to their portfolio, and McColl's Coaches Ltd was dissolved in May, but operations continued under the McColl's commercial repairs licence.

As can be seen, the number of operators that have disappeared is phenomenal. The above is not intended to be a full list of service changes, but to give a flavour of happenings over the years.

Fans arrive at Celtic Park to the chant of, 'Get your hats, scarves and flags here.' Paton's no. 100, EJY 354, has just disgorged its supporters on a patch of waste ground used for parking the buses. It was an all-Leyland Titan PD2/1 L27/26R, new as Plymouth Corporation no. 354 in October 1949, which joined Paton's in February 1966 and lasted until January 1968. No. 100 was the highest fleet number ever reached as the sequence began again at no. 1.

Lowland Motorways began in 1928 with long-distance operations that later passed to Alexanders. A coach fleet was then built up under the Greyhound title and in 1952 the business Harry Black of Springboig was purchased and this was a springboard for services in the east end of Glasgow. Dealer Millburn Motors took a 50 per cent shareholding and would provide good second-hand stock over the years. JXC 181 was a Cravens-bodied AEC Regent and would pass to Scottish Omnibuses with the business on 13 January 1958, becoming fleet number BB1.

HHA 157L was a Leyland National 1151/1R B52F purchased new by Midland Red as their no. 157 in July 1973. On disposal it passed to the British Airports Authority before purchase by Weir's Tours. It is seen in an attractive setting as it arrives in Helensburgh. The company was owned by Dennis Noble, who had originally traded as Mallard Coaches but changed to Weir's Tours after purchasing the goodwill of Weir's Tours of Bowling.

G217 HCP was a DAF SB220/Optare Delta B49F purchased new by Smith's of Alcester in February 1990. It passed to Travel West Midlands with the business before sale to Russell Arden in 2002, and was captured in Cambridge Street in Glasgow. Even before the business was sold to West Coast Motors, there had been plans to change the livery to a yellow front end with the rest of the bus in red.

The spire of Glasgow University towers above McGill's YY64 YKH. This ADL Enviro is one of many new buses recently introduced to the fleet, and presents a very smart image to the travelling public. McGill's is the largest independent in Scotland nowadays, with a fleet of around 450 vehicles, and will be dealt with more thoroughly in a separate volume in the series. The purchase of Arriva's Scottish operations doubled the size of the fleet overnight in March 2012.

BSG 551W was a Leyland Tiger TRCTL11/3R, new as a Duple-bodied coach to Eastern Scottish (XH 551) in July 1981. It was re-bodied for Allander's Loch Lomond fleet by East Lancs with a B53F EL2000 bus body in May 1993. It was sold to Rossendale Transport (no. 74) in 1997, and was later re-registered as PJI 9174. Dumbarton High Street provides the backdrop, with shops such as Woolworths and Malcolm Campbell now but a distant memory.

RBU 180R was a Leyland National 11351A/1R B49F purchased new by Greater Manchester PTE as their no. 180 in March 1977. It passed to Chesterfield Transport (no. 82) and with the business became part of Stagecoach East Midland. It joined Dart Buses of Paisley in 1997 and was caught in Wellington Street in Glasgow city centre. It would only carry this registration briefly before being re-registered as NIL 5368. Sadly, the Dart business collapsed overnight in October 2001.

G756 SRB was a Scania N113CRB/Alexander PS Type B51F, purchased new by Nottingham City Transport as their no. 756. It was latterly a driver trainer and part of the lettering was incorporated into its livery with McColl's. It was caught in Chalmers Street in Clydebank working on the 204 service. This livery was most impractical and very difficult to keep clean, and was superseded by a version of the old Duncan Stewart colours.

T500 CBC was a Dennis Dart SLF/Marshall B43F, new in April 1999 to Coakley of Motherwell. It is seen with City Sprinter as T731 DGD, crossing Glasgow's Jamaica Bridge on service 38 to Eastwood Toll. Alan Arnott took a pair of these Darts in 2003, which were priced at £45,000 each at the time. They didn't last long, however, as they didn't justify a good enough return on that sort of investment, and were returned to the dealer, Blythswood Motors, before this one joined South Lancs Transport.

LUA 324V was a Leyland National 2 B41F, new in March 1980 to West Yorkshire PTE. It was sold to Stevenson's of Uttoxeter (no. 132), then went to Somerbus of Paulton in 1992, spending just a year there before joining Canavan's in 1993. It is seen on service 89, which ran from Kirkintilloch to Glasgow using the same timings that Green's had used. It would later run for Marchant's of Cheltenham.

GSN 514L was a fine Daimler Fleetline CRG6LX/Alexander AL Type H43/31F, purchased new by Garelochhead Coach Services as their no. 107 in June 1973. I always thought the narrow destination box let it down a little. It seems very strange now to see the simple phone number, 'phone 200', introduced long before all the national dialling codes. Sadly the business ceased in 1980, with this bus seeing further service with Inverclyde of Greenock.

YVV 896S was a Bristol VRT/SL3/6LXB/ECW H74F purchased new by United Counties as their no. 896 in June 1978. It passed to Cambus as their 673 before running for Red Kite of Tilsworth. It then joined Green's of Kirkintilloch and is seen turning into St Vincent Street in Glasgow as it heads for its terminus at Anderston bus station.

M753 WWR was an Optare Metrorider MR31 B25F, purchased new by Selby & District (no. 753) in April 1995. It passed to Arriva Yorkshire and later Arriva Scotland West before joining McGill's of Greenock. On disposal it passed to Localink of Barrhead, t/a A&P Coaches, and is seen working on the short-lived service 55, which connected the city to Braehead. It would later see further service with First Stop Travel.

S521 KFL was a Dennis Dart SLF/Marshall C39 B32F, new as Metroline London Northern no. DMS21 in August 1998. In May 2003 it was fitted with wheelchair ramp and CCTV and down-seated to B28F. On disposal in July 2008 it was acquired by Galleon Travel of Harlow. It moved to M Travel, based at Old Trafford, in March 2009 then passed to Pilkington's of Accrington in July 2010. It was bought by City Sprinter of Renfrew in March 2011 and ran for two years. This view shows it in Kilmarnock Road near Giffnock.

Glasgow Citybus ADL Enviro 200 YX12 DJJ is shown passing Crookston Castle on the Sunday-only service 153, which connects Cessnock to Silverburn Shopping Centre. The castle is surrounded by a defensive ring-ditch that dates back to the twelfth century when Sir Robert de Croc, who also gave his name to the village of Crookston, built a timber and earth castle. The Citybus fleet is garaged in South Street in Glasgow.

OJD 412R was a Leyland Fleetline FE30ALR/Park Royal H44/24D, new as London Transport DMS2412 in May 1977. It was purchased by the Big Bus Co. for London sightseeing in July 1992, and converted to open-top in June 1994. It passed to PD Travel of Glasgow and was used on Glasgow sightseeing tours from June 2007. The tour ran for two seasons before the company ceased all operations.

USO 189S was a Ford R1114/Alexander Y Type B53F, purchased new by Alexander (Northern) as their NT189 in January 1978. On disposal it passed to Cameron of Alexandria, t/a Castle Coaches, and is seen in Alexandria. It had been supplied by the Regal Coaches dealership owned by Green's of Kirkintilloch, and would return there before joining Arthur Woodcock's AD Coaches, based in Dundonald.

K604 ESH was a Dennis Dart 9.8SDL/Alexander Dash B40F, purchased new as Fife Scottish no. 604 in August 1992. On disposal in 2006 it joined the PD Travel fleet, and is seen in Chalmers Street in Clydebank. PD Travel, Beta Buses and Go Diesel were all trading names of Bayview Enterprises, who were based in Helensburgh.

DPW 783T was a Leyland National 11351A/1R B49F, purchased new by Eastern Counties as their no. LN783 in February 1979. It passed to Cambus before joining Green's and is leading sister DPW 784T into Glasgow's Anderston bus station. It would pass to Kelvin Central Buses with the services and become no. 1124. Green's were bidding for batches of buses and using some from their own fleet and selling on to other operators.

On your marks! Three sadly missed independents meet for a couple of seconds at the traffic lights in Glasgow city centre at the junction of Argyle Street and Union Street. On the left we have Dart of Paisley, middle lane Gibson Direct of Renfrew, and on the right Mckindless of Wishaw, all about to go in different directions. Unfortunately none of these companies survived running bus services but Gibson's have re-invented themselves in the field of coach hires and contracts.

H141 MOB was a Dennis Dart/Carlyle Dartline B28F, new as London Buses no. DT141 in January 1991. It passed to Metroline in October 1994, and on disposal in November 1998 joined Independent Way, t/a Limebourne of London. It was transferred to Excalibur Coach Co. of Battersea in July 2001. In May 2003 it was bought by Beta Buses, and was later moved to the associated PD Travel fleet. It was bought by Caledonia of Glasgow in June 2004, and caught in Union Street working a journey on service 44.

G874 SKE was a Talbot Pullman B22F, new as Kentish Bus & Coach no. 874 in December 1989. It passed to Ashton Coaches of Port Glasgow in 1996, and was acquired by City Sprinter two years later. Although cheap to buy, these buses proved to be unreliable and were ultimately replaced by Mercedes minibuses. Under later ownership the company ended operations after it was found that buses were running without insurance.

P611 CMS was a Dennis Dart/Alexander Dash B40F, delivered new as Stagecoach Fife no. 611 in August 1996. On disposal in 2010 it joined Colchri Coaches and was passing Elder Park in Govan while working on the 23 service, which competed with the Firstbus service carrying the same number. The company name came from the owner's children's names, which were COLin and CHRIstine.

YN07 LHV was a Scania N230UD/East Lancs H68D, purchased new by London United (no. SO5) in June 2007. It was purchased by Glasgow Citybus and used very briefly in service before passing to the associated Sightseeing Glasgow fleet and converted to partial open-top for use on city tours. It was snapped as it turned into Renfield Street while working on the 17 service.

PHA 307M was a Leyland Leopard PSU3B/4R/Plaxton Elite C44Ft, purchased new by Midland Red as their no. 307 in April 1974. On disposal it passed to John Boyce Coaches and then Duncan Stewart's, where it operated as a forty-nine-seater. It then passed to Donald Bagley, t/a DEB Travel, and is seen on the short-lived service linking Glasgow and Eaglesham. Very heavy duplication by the low-cost GCT unit of Strathclyde Buses saw the service withdrawn after only six months. The bus would then pass to Nelson's of Thornhill.

SN51 UCR was a Dennis Dart SLF/Alexander ALX200 B29F, purchased new in January 2002 by Richmond of Epsom, t/a Epsom Buses (Quality Line), as their no. SD35. It was acquired by John Morrow and is passing through Chalmers Street in Clydebank. It would later run for Proctors, t/a Leven Valley of Middlesbrough, as their no. 73.

Y285 FJN was a Dennis Dart SLF/Alexander ALX200 B30D, delivered new to Stagecoach East London as their no. SLD285 in August 2001. It became no. DM285 in 2002, then was renumbered into the national fleet numbering scheme as no. 34285 in 2003. The business was sold to the East London Bus Group in June 2006, and on disposal in July 2011 McColl's of Balloch purchased the bus. It became McGill's of Greenock no. 4766 after McColl's sold their services in January 2013.

DWH 696W was a Leyland Fleetline FE30AGR/Northern Counties H43/32F, purchased new by Lancashire United as their no. 603 in November 1980. It passed to Green's of Kirkintilloch and was working on the city to Waterside service. It was lent to Beaton's of Blantyre for a couple of weeks in 1991 before sale to Dunnet's of Keiss. It passed to Rapson's with the services and later joined the Highland fleet in 1992.

KMA 408T was a Leyland National 11351A/1R B49F, purchased new by Crosville as their no. SNL408 in April 1979. It was one of nearly 100 buses converted to Gardner engines in the early 1980s, and was transferred to Crosville Wales when the company was split. It passed to McColl's and was passing through Dumbarton on the D5 service. It would become Kelvin Central Buses no. 1130 in August 1992 after McColl's sold their services.

K103 OMW was a Dennis Dart 8.5SDL/Plaxton Pointer B33F, delivered new as Thamesdown no. 103 in February 1993. On disposal it passed to Law's of Tetbury before reaching Puma Coaches of Glasgow in 2004, and was leaving Govan bus station on the 23 service, heading for Pollok. Puma Coaches was owned by Anthony Morrin, who had previously worked for Clydeside Scottish at Thornliebank depot.

SN51 TCU is a Dennis Dart SLF/Plaxton Pointer B30D, purchased new by London United as their no. DPS600 in December 2001. It joined Avondale in 2013 and is seen in Chalmers Street in Clydebank. With the launch of the Dennis Dart in 1989, Plaxton's subsidiary Reeve Burgess made the Pointer body on the short 8.5-metre chassis. Launched in 1991, this proved popular with many operators, and they sold in big numbers in London. The introduction of the Super Low Floor (SLF) version of the Dennis Dart, the Dart SLF, in 1995 saw the Pointer body redesigned with a 2.4-metre width, with a step-free entrance, giving easy access for the disabled.

SN11 BVF is an ADL Enviro 200 Hybrid B37F, purchased new by Colchri Coaches of Renfrew in July 2011. It is shown fully repainted on the newly introduced service H2, which connects Silverburn and the Queen Elizabeth University Hospital. A hybrid electric bus combines a conventional internal combustion engine propulsion system with an electric propulsion system. These types of buses normally use a diesel-electric powertrain.

SF54 ORJ was an Optare Solo M850 B20F, purchased new in October 2004 by Gibson's of Renfrew for use on SPT dial-a-bus services. It was one of four later lent to City Sprinter and was captured as it crossed Jamaica Bridge in Glasgow. It returned to Gibson's and was sold to Ayrways of Ayr for further service. The Solo has been manufactured by Optare in the United Kingdom since 1998, and its name is a play on its low-floor status, that is 'so low'.

H140 MOB was a Dennis Dart/Carlyle B28F, purchased new by London Buses in January 1990 as their no. DT140. It passed to privatised Metroline in October 1994. Dealer Fleetmaster in Horsham purchased it in February 2001 and fitted it with a Plaxton Pointer front end to cure the Carlyle body's biggest weakness – incredibly, the front windscreen protruded further than the bumper! Anglian of Beccles purchased it in July 2001 and ran it until July 2002. It passed to Gibson's of Renfrew and was pressed into service in its former livery. By August 2003 it was with Beta Buses of Alexandria, owned by Phil Docherty, although it would carry PD Travel fleet names.

YJ03 PGF was a DAF SB120/Wright Cadet B39F, purchased new by Glasgow Citybus in May 2003. It was supplied by dealers Arriva and is seen turning into Glasgow's Argyle Street while working on the 17 service, which connected the city to Duntocher. It was later transferred to West Coast Motors' Rothesay depot and would receive WCM livery.

TWH 697T was a Leyland Fleetline FE30AGR/Northern Counties H75F, new to Lancashire United as their no. 522. It was renumbered to no. 6938 but was involved in a low bridge accident. It was decided to rebuild it as a twenty-eight-seater single-decker renumbered no. 1697. On disposal it passed to Green's of Kirkintilloch, then John Morrow of Clydebank, before reaching Kelvin Central Buses. After disposal it ran very briefly for Pringle of Bearsden on the Glasgow sightseeing tour but was not really suitable and was used for spares for their fleet of open-top Fleetline double-deckers.

VPT 946R was a Leyland National 11351A/1R B49F, purchased new by United in March 1977. It was originally intended to be East Midland 3046 but was diverted before delivery took place. On disposal it passed to dealer Regal in Kirkintilloch before purchase by Canavan of Croy. It then joined McColl's Coaches, who were based in Dalmuir at that time. The livery was intended to match the very large batch of Atlanteans purchased from Greater Manchester Transport.

This Leyland Leopard PSU5C/4R/Alexander T Type B51F was new to Singapore Bus Services in September 1979 as BS6791. It returned to the UK in 1982 to dealer Paul Sykes, before joining the fleet of Woods of Mirfield (Gobig Ltd). Allander of Milngavie bought it for their Loch Lomond bus services division in May 1989 and it was photographed in Balloch. Allander had it re-bodied in May 1992 with a new Plaxton Derwent 2 B57F body. On disposal it passed to Finglands of Rusholme, then went to Ireland, joining the fleet of Kavanagh's of Tipperary before being scrapped in 2007.

N202 WSB was one of a pair of Dennis Darts bought new by Oban & District while still in independent ownership. They passed to West Coast Motors when they took over in 1999 and proved excellent and reliable workhorses, this particular one ending its days in the Glasgow Citybus fleet. It is seen here on Kilbowie Road in Clydebank.

K718 DAO was a Volvo B10M-55/Alexander PS Type B49F, new to Stagecoach Cumberland (no. 718) in December 1996. It was transferred to Stagecoach Western in 2003 and was used in Magicbus livery against Ayrways services, later receiving standard fleet livery and being renumbered to no. 20718. On disposal it passed to McColl's and is seen in Balloch in this view. It would later pass to Rigby's Coaches, then DJ International when McColl's decided to go low-floor.

A flavour of the myriad of colours that the independents brought to the area is evident in this shot, taken in Chalmers Street in Clydebank. Only Avondale have survived, but minibuses have given way to a fleet of low-floor Darts and Solos. The McKindless group collapsed overnight on 19 February 2010, and John Morrow retired on 31 March 2010.

M870 DYS was a Volvo B6-50/Alexander Dash B40F new to Allander's Loch Lomond fleet in October 1994. It passed to Kelvin Central with the business and has seen service with KCB, GCT, First Glasgow and First Eastern Counties. It was caught in Dumbarton High Street while heading for Balloch on the D6 service.

PJJ 350S was a Leyland National 10351A/1R B41F, purchased new by East Kent as their no. 1350 in October 1977. John Morrow acquired it in 1989 for use on the inter-station service and it wore Strathclyde PTE red but with a yellow front added. It was leaving Glasgow Central station, which was opened by the Caledonian Railway on 1 August 1879.

F68 RFS was an MCW Metrorider MF150/102 DP25F, delivered new as Fife Scottish no. 68 in August 1988. On disposal it joined Skyline Travel Services, owned by Frank Dolan, who was also a junior partner in Puma Coaches and later Colchri up until 2009. It was leaving Govan bus station on the 23 service to Pollok.

A pair of ex-London Darts meets briefly in Glasgow. McKindless L164 XRH was new as London Buses no. DRL164 in January 1994, while City Sprinter M103 BLE was new as Metroline no. EDR3 in October 1994. Both carried Plaxton Pointer bodywork built at Scarborough. The design was originally built by Reeves Burgess, which was a Plaxton subsidiary. In August 2006 Alexander Dennis launched the Enviro200 Dart as a replacement for the Pointer Dart.

R116 NTA was a Mercedes O814D/Alexander ALX100 B25F, purchased new by Devon General as their no. 116 in July 1998. It was the last in a batch of fourteen of these Varios, and would become no. 42116 in the Stagecoach fleet before it and many sister vehicles later transferred north to Scotland. Two saw use with City Sprinter on the south side of Glasgow and three saw service with Avondale in Clydebank.

L509 OAL was a Volvo B6-50/Alexander Dash B40F, delivered new as Nottingham City Transport no. 509 in May 1994. It was purchased by Dave Bishop, trading as DB Travel, and is passing along Chalmers Street in Clydebank on the 62 service bound for Partick. On the demise of DB in November 2008, it would pass to City Sprinter for further service.

OUC 48R was a Leyland Fleetline FE30AGR/MCW H68D, new to London Transport as DMS 2048 in December 1976. It passed to Graham's Bus Service of Paisley (no. D2) in March 1984 and was rebuilt to H76F before entering service. In February 1988 it joined Duncan Stewart's fleet at Dalmuir. McColl's Coaches kept it when the Duncan Stewart consortium finished in August 1991. In February 1992 it was sold to Kerr's of Galston and it remained in Ayrshire with Shuttle Buses of Kilwinning from August 1994 to August 1996, when it passed to Dunsmore of Larkhall for scrap. This view shows it turning in Clydebank to begin a new journey to Balloch.

M702 RVS was a MAN 11.190/Optare Vecta B40F, purchased new by Seamarks of Luton in September 1994. It was acquired by Singh of Huddersfield before joining the Morrow fleet in 2000. It moved to Fairbrother of Warrington before passing to G. H. Watts of Leicester, where it would be re-registered as NXI 608. This view shows the four-square advert for McDonalds' Clydebank branch.

R557 UOT was a Dennis Dart SLF/UVG B44F, delivered new to Marchwood Motorways of Totton as their no. 557 in August 1997. On disposal it joined Teamdeck of Honley, t/a K-Line, as their no. 18. It was acquired by Glasgow Citybus in 2005, and this view shows it at Summerston in a contract livery for ASDA Stores.

M721BCS was a Volvo B6-50/Alexander Dash DP40F purchased new by Stagecoach Western in July 1994. It is seen in Glasgow city centre working for Alan Arnott's City Sprinter fleet. It will be noted that it still carries its Ferrymill (dealer) fleet number, FM12. This was not the first time that it had operated route 38 in Glasgow as Dickson's of Erskine had also ran the bus briefly, on loan from Ferrymill Motors.

K225 VTB was a Dennis Dart/Northern Counties Paladin new to Warrington Borough Transport as their fleet number 225 in September 1992. It passed to Avondale in 2004 and is seen in Chalmers Street in Clydebank. The Paladin body was built in Wigan between 1991 and 1998. Plaxton took over Northern Counties and replaced this model with the Pointer.

JDZ 2409 was a Dennis Dart 9SDL/Wright Handybus B35F new as London Buses no. DWL9 in December 1990. It passed to the privatised Westlink company in January 1994, and to London United from December 1997. On disposal in November 2001 it was acquired by Lionspeed, t/a Pete's Travel, based in West Bromwich, before joining Caledonian of Glasgow in August 2003. It entered service in its previous livery, but received Caledonian red in due course.

DN02 EDN was a Transbus Enviro 300 B44F, delivered new to Truronian of Truro in August 2000. It was re-registered as KW02 DSE and passed to New Concept Coaches, which was associated with Caledonian, for use on the Glasgow Airport service. It later worked for Weavaway of Newbury before reaching Blue Diamond in the West Midlands as their no. 30492.

LEU 258P was a Bristol VRT/SL3/6LXB/ECW H43/27D, purchased new by Bristol Omnibus as their fleet number C5050 in June 1976. On disposal it passed to Circle Line of Gloucester before purchase by John Morrow. Six of these buses were acquired, but not all entered service before the company was sold to Kelvin Central Buses. This one was turning at Lincoln Avenue as it headed for Faifley.

X83 AAK was a MAN 18.220/Ikarus Polaris B42F, built as a demonstrator for MAN Bus & Coach, Swindon, in December 2000. It was sold to Bennett's of Gloucester before joining McColl's of Balloch, where it received SPT livery for use on tendered services. It then passed to Staffwise of Portsmouth and finally Isle Coaches of Owston Ferry before being sold for scrap.

YOT 545V was a Leyland National NL116L11/2R B44D, new as Gosport & Fareham no. 45 in May 1980. It is shown with Crainey's of Kilsyth and would later pass to Aintree Coachlines, K-Line of Huddersfield and eventually Leask of Lerwick in 1993. The slogan on the front, 'Myles better bus', refers to the owner's name.

WST 79V was a Bristol LHS6L/ECW DP27F, purchased new by Westerbus of Badcaul in November 1979. It passed to Ann's Coaches of Kirkintilloch before reaching Allander Travel's Loch Lomond Coaches fleet, and is seen near Balloch on the service to Balmaha. Allander Travel was established in 1960 as a taxi operator, but moved into coaches in 1967.

96-D-206 was a Volvo Olympian/Alexander R Type, new as Dublin Bus RA206 in 1995. On disposal in 2008 it joined McColl's Commercial Repairs Ltd as their fleet number 3033. It was technically owned by City Tours (Glasgow) Ltd, which was another McColl-owned company. At one time both McColl's and PJ Travel had an interest in this firm, but it became wholly owned by McColl's.

DOC 41V was a Leyland National NL116L11/1R B50F, new to West Midlands PTE as their fleet number 1041 in June 1980. It passed to Teamdeck of Horley (perhaps better known as K-Line) before joining Glasgow Citybus in 2000 and is seen running on service 17, about to turn into Hope Street in Glasgow. It was later preserved back into WMPTE livery with WJC Coaches and was fitted with a DAF engine.

There was a brief period in 2006 when First Glasgow's 38 service was being attacked at both ends by different operators. The southern section was being challenged by City Sprinter. However, for a while, the northern section was also under attack between the city and Garthamlock by Canavan Coaches, in retaliation for a Firstbus incursion in the Cumbernauld area.

NFM 842M was a Leyland National 1151/1R/0405 DP48F, new as Crosville fleet number ENL842 in November 1973. It was acquired by John Morrow and is shown in Argyle Street in Glasgow, working on the tendered SECC circular 100 service. It would pass to Kelvin Central Buses with the services in 1992, although John would retain a small coach fleet.

SN15 AKY is one of a pair of B31F Wright StreetLites delivered to Wilson's of Rhu in June 2015, and was working on service 316, which connects Helensburgh to Coulport. The StreetLite is a low-floor midibus introduced by Wrightbus in 2010. It was originally available in only one body style (wheel forward) before the door forward and StreetLite Max variants were introduced in 2011 and 2012 respectively.

JUS 790N was a Leyland Atlantean AN68/1R/Alexander AL Type H45/31F, new as Greater Glasgow PTE no. LA943 in July 1975. It was sold to Lonsdale Coaches in Heysham before passing to Crainey's of Kilsyth. It was working on the joint Crainey/Canavan service linking Glasgow and Kirkintilloch.

R551 UOT was a Dennis Dart SLF/UVG B44F, delivered new to Marchwood Motorways of Totton as their no. 551 in August 1997. On disposal it joined Teamdeck of Honley, t/a K-Line. It was acquired by Glasgow Citybus in 2005 and repainted, but this view shows it in the later West Coast Motors-inspired version of the livery as it turns into Argyle Street.

WSU 448S was a Leyland Leopard PSU3C/4R/ Alexander Y Type B53F purchased new by Central SMT as their T306 in November 1977. It passed to Kelvin Central Buses (no. 1448) in 1989 and was given a full repaint before its sale to Loch Lomond a week later. It was captured in Dumbarton. On disposal it passed to Marbill of Beith for further service.

T415 LGP was a Dennis Dart SLF/Caetano B31D, purchased new by Independent Way of Battersea, t/a Limbourne, in May 1999, later becoming part of Connex London. It passed to Caledonian of Glasgow in 2005. It later worked for Faresaver of Chippenham before ending up with Falkland Islands Tours and Travel with the registration number F189J.

SN56 AYA was an ADL Enviro 200 B29F built as a demonstrator for Alexander Dennis, Falkirk, in October 2006. In 2009 it passed to Colchri Coaches and is seen in Pollok. It subsequently moved to JP Coaches of Forfar before passing to McGill's of Greenock as their fleet number H8433.

H166 NON was a Dennis Dart 8.5SDL/Carlyle B28F, new as London Buses no. DT166 in February 1991. It joined the privatised London United company in November 1994. It was acquired by the fledgling Glasgow Citybus fleet set up by Russell Arden, and is seen in Clydebank. The company was sold to West Coast Motors in January 2006, and this little bus was cannibalised for spares.

R964 XVM is a Volvo B10M-55/Alexander PS Type B49F, purchased new by Greater Manchester South (no. 964) in November 1997. It became Stagecoach Manchester no. 20964 and saw service with Stagecoach Strathtay before reaching Garelochhead Coaches for use as a school bus. It was photographed in Arrochar.

PRA 12R was a Leyland Leopard PSU3C/4R/ Alexander T Type C49F, new as East Midland no. 12 in November 1976. It was transferred to United, and passed with the Scarborough operations to Scarborough & District. It was acquired by Allander Travel for their Loch Lomond fleet and was snapped in Dumbarton.

GPJ 891N was a Leyland National 11351/1R B49F, new as Alder Valley no. 191 in March 1975. It was re-bodied by East Lancs in August 1994 and operated for Pilkington's of Accrington before reaching John Morrow, and is seen in Clydebank. On disposal it would pass to Lewis's Coaches of Llanrhystud.

ANJ 309T was a Leyland Leopard PSU3E/4RT/Plaxton Supreme C49F, purchased new by Southdown as their no. 1309 in November 1978. On disposal it was one of a batch acquired by Rennie's of Dunfermline, before sale to First Stop Travel, and was working on their Glasgow city centre to Penilee Service. It received a set of seats out of a DMU train, which had latterly been fitted in former Strathclyde Leopard JGE 30T.

J24 MCW was a Volvo B10M-50/East Lancs B45F delivered new as Burnley & Pendle no. 24 in February 1992. It passed to Stagecoach with the business and was later transferred to Stagecoach Western. It became McColl's no. 1001, and was unloading passengers in Chalmers Street in Clydebank.

K416 MGN was a Dennis Dart/Plaxton Pointer B36F, new to R&I Tours of London as their no. 236 in March 1993. It passed to Metroline with the business and became no. DP236 before sale to Alan Thomson's Caledonia Buses fleet in 2003. It was caught turning from Union Street into Argyle Street while working a service 66 to Busby.

J604 KCU was a Dennis Dart/Wright Handybus B40F, new to Go Ahead Northern-owned Tyneside Omnibus Co. (no. 8004) in December 1991. It was one of a batch purchased by Dart Buses and operated under a franchise agreement for Stagecoach Glasgow. The X8/9/10 had been very successful when launched but passenger numbers had been steadily declining, mainly because high-density housing was being demolished. As a cost-cutting measure Dart was sub-contracted to operate these services on behalf of Stagecoach and many non-low-floor buses replaced modern Stagecoach vehicles.

D377 RHS was a Volvo B10M-61/Duple Dominant B55F, new to Hutchison's in June 1987. It would remain in the fleet until 1993, when it was sold to Allander Coaches of Milngavie for their Loch Lomond Bus Services operations. It then passed to Whitelaw's of Stonehouse for further service in June 1996 and remained there until sold to John Morrow of Clydebank in February 2008. It is shown freshly repainted at Dumbarton.

This Ford R192/Willowbrook DP45F was new in October 1971 to Garelochhead Coach Services and was supplied by S&N Motors, the Glasgow-based Ford dealers. It is seen in Helensburgh, beside the railway station, in July 1974, screened up for its next journey back to its home village. Sadly the company ceased operations in 1980.

J952 MFT was a Dennis Dart 9.8SDL/Wright Handybus B40F new as Northern General no. 8052 in August 1992. On disposal it joined Dennis's of Dunkinfield as their no. DW12. First Stop Travel under the ownership of Slaemuir Coaches acquired it and repainted it. It would pass to McKindless of Wishaw in 2006.

TSD 611S was a Leyland Atlantean AN68A/1R/Alexander AL Type H45/33F, purchased new by A1 Service member John McMenemy in November 1977, and was basically to Glasgow spec. On disposal it passed to Rennie's of Dunfermline, then saw further service with Canavan of Croy, East Yorkshire and OK Motor Services. It is shown working a peak-hour express out of Glasgow.

K574 LTS was a Volvo B10M-55/Alexander PS Type B49F, new as Stagecoach Scotland no. 574 in April 1993. It later saw service with Stagecoach Glasgow. McColl's purchased it in 2009 and numbered it as their no. 2012. It is shown arriving in Glasgow city centre on the 204 service, with a similar Firstbus vehicle in hot pursuit.

A509 EJF was acquired by Colchri Coaches in 2014 for use on school contracts, but it made the odd foray onto the company's stage-carriage operations and was captured on Barrhead Road in Glasgow. It is a Leyland Olympian ONLXB/1R/ECW H77F, purchased new by Midland Fox as their no. 4509 in November 1983. It passed to Arriva Midlands, and on disposal went to Country Hopper of Ibstock.

H141 MOB was a Dennis Dart/Carlyle Dartline B28F, new as London Buses no. DT141 in January 1991. It passed to Metroline in October 1994, and on disposal in November 1998 joined Independent Way, t/a Limebourne of London. It was transferred to Excalibur Coach Co., Battersea, in July 2001. In May 2003 it was bought by Beta Buses, and was moved to the associated PD Travel fleet. Ingram Street in Glasgow provides the backdrop for this view while working on the service to Clydebank. It passed to Caledonia Buses of Glasgow in June 2004.

L505 OAL was a Volvo B6-50/ Alexander Dash B40F, new as Nottingham City Transport no. 505 in May 1994. On disposal it joined DB Travel briefly before sale to City Sprinter. It was heading along Eglinton Street on the firm's 38 service, bound for Eastwood Toll. Stagecoach Western and Firstbus also served this busy corridor.

R551 UOT was a Dennis Dart SLF/UVG B44F, delivered new to Marchwood Motorways of Totton as their no. 551 in August 1997. On disposal it joined Teamdeck of Honley, t/a K-Line. It was acquired by Glasgow Citybus in 2005 and was pressed into service in its former owner's colours, but would quickly receive fleet livery.

KX07 KNY was an Enterprise EB01/Plaxton Primo B28F, purchased new by Colchri Coaches of Renfrew in August 2007, and is seen near Giffnock. The Plaxton Primo was a small low-floor bus body based on the Enterprise Bus Plasma chassis. It was launched by Plaxton in 2005. The fully welded stainless steel integral chassis final assembly was supplied in right-hand drive format as a running unit to Plaxton. Final body assembly was undertaken by Plaxton in Scarborough.

YJ15 AXU is an Optare
Solo SR M710SE B20F,
purchased new by Glasgow
Citybus in March 2015. It
was captured turning into
Brockburn Road in Pollok.
3,857 original model Solos
were built between 1998
and 2012, and as of April
2017, almost 1,500 Solo
SRs have been built. The
chassis type code of the Solo
denotes the length – M710
corresponds to 7.1 metres,
M780 to 7.8 metres, M850
to 8.5 metres, and so forth.

LG02 FGU was a Dennis
Dart SLF/Plaxton Pointer
B30D, purchased new by
London United as their
fleet number DPS667
in July 2002. It operated
in Glasgow for City
Sprinter and was bound
for Castlemilk on the
short-lived service 75.
This area of the Gorbals
has since been extensively
redeveloped.

Y969 TGH is a Dennis
Dart SLF/Plaxton Pointer
B29F, purchased new by
London Central as their
no. LDP169 in April 2001.
On disposal in March
2012 it passed to Avondale
Coaches and is seen in
Clydebank. Conveniently,
this view shows both the
back and front of the
Pointer bodywork.

TWH 697T was a Leyland Fleetline FE30AGR/Northern Counties H75F, new to Lancashire United as their no. 522. It was renumbered to no. 6938 but was involved in a low bridge accident. It was decided to rebuild it as a twenty-eight-seater single-decker renumbered no. 1697. On disposal it passed to Green's of Kirkintilloch, then John Morrow of Clydebank, before reaching Kelvin Central Buses. After disposal it ran very briefly for Pringle of Bearsden on the Glasgow sightseeing tour but was not really suitable and was used for spares for their fleet of open-top Fleetline double-deckers.

T419 KAG was a Dennis Dart SLF/Plaxton Pointer B27D, new as London United fleet number DP19 in March 1999. On disposal it was bought by McNairn's of Coatbridge for some new services in the Motherwell area launched in 2011. It was bought by City Sprinter of Renfrew in March 2012, and was crossing the River Clyde at Jamaica Bridge in Glasgow.

YYE 279T was a Leyland National 10351A/2R B36D, purchased new as London Transport LS279 in March 1979. John Morrow purchased it in 1990, and it is seen passing through Clydebank on the service to Linnvale. Problems keeping the livery looking clean led to the introduction of dark brown roofs on later repaints.

NCS 117W was a Volvo B10M-61/Duple Dominant III C46Ft, purchased new by Western Scottish in June 1981 for use on the Scotland to London service. It would pass to Clydeside Scottish as their no. 417 and was rebuilt to Dominant IV style. After an eventful life it was sold to Allander of Milngavie for their Loch Lomond fleet and re-bodied with an East Lancs service bus body in August 1992.

YJ15 ASU is an Optare Solo M8900SR, purchased new by Garelochhead Coaches in May 2015, and was snapped in West Princes Street in Helensburgh. The fleet numbers around eighteen vehicles and is kept up to date. A mixture of school contracts, coach hire and service work is operated, including the tendered service in Glasgow linking the Transport Museum, SECC and city centre.

M227 VSX was a Volvo Olympian YN2R/Alexander RH Type H51/30D new, as Lothian Buses no. 227 in June 1995. It was acquired by West Coast Motors, but lent to their Glasgow Citybus subsidiary in 2009. It was working on the 17 service, bound for Duntocher, when captured in Argyle Street in Glasgow.

AML 645H was an AEC Merlin 4P2R/MCW B50F, new as London Transport no. MB645 in October 1969. It was purchased by Garelochhead Coach Services as their fleet number 137 in May 1977. It was prepared for service by Dodd's of Troon, which explains the dark green applied instead of the light green usually associated with this fleet. It passed to dealer Trevor Wigley of Carlton for scrap in December 1980.

BOK 78V was an MCW Metrobus DR102 H73F, new to West Midlands PTE as their fleet number 2078 in June 1980. It passed to McColl's in 1999 and is seen passing through Dumbarton town centre on its way to Balloch. McColl's were putting in tenders for batches of redundant vehicles at this time, and purchased many from the West Midlands.

LPT 903P was a Leyland Leopard PSU3C/4R/Willowbook B55F, purchased new by Trimdon Motor Services in August 1975. On disposal it passed to Silcox of Pembroke Dock, then Thorne's of Bubwith before joining Loch Lomond Coaches in 1988. It ran for around a year before being dispatched to Willowbrook for a new Warrior body. This view shows it in Dumbarton while still fitted with its original bodywork.

VCD 292S was a Leyland Leopard PSU3E/4R/Duple Dominant C47F, purchased new by Southdown as their fleet number 1292 in January 1978. On disposal it passed to Rennie's of Dunfermline, and was fitted with a later style of front end before sale to Canavan of Croy. It was captured in Wellington Street in Glasgow working on the service to Harestanes.

YT11 LSE was a Scania N230UD Omnidekka H45/31F, built as a demonstrator for Scania Worksop in June 2011. It was purchased by West Coast for use on Mull, but was on loan to Glasgow Citybus to add extra capacity around Christmas 2016. It has since been transferred to West Coast's Dunoon depot.

GLS 287N was a Leyland Leopard PSU3/3R / Alexander Y Type B53F, purchased new by Alexander (Midland) as their MPE 217 in November 1974. It was acquired by John Morrow and is seen at Mountblow. John had worked for Midland at Milngavie depot in earlier years, and knew the buses were well maintained.

S581 PGB was a Dennis Dart MPD /Plaxton Pointer B29F, new to Canavan of Croy in December 1998. On disposal in 2006 it passed to Gibson Direct, then passed to McGill's with the services in May 2011. This view shows it new in Cumbernauld.

H335 DHA was a Renault S56/Northern Counties B23F, purchased new by Midland Red North as their no. 335 in December 1990. It passed to John Walker and ran briefly for Scotway in its original livery. It was later re-painted into orange for the associated Local Bus Company and was snapped in Glasgow city centre.

UGE 389W was a Leyland National NL116AL11/1R B52F, purchased new by McGill's of Barrhead in April 1981. It passed with the business into Arriva ownership in July 1997 as no. 777. It was lent to Dart Buses of Paisley in early 1999, then sold to Essbee of Coatbridge in March 1999. By November 2000 it had moved to Camden Coaches of West Kingsdown.

G54 TGW was a Dennis Dart 8.5SDL/Carlyle B28F, new as London Buses no. DT54 in July 1990. In November 1994 it became part of the privatised London United fleet. On disposal in November 1999 it passed to McKindless of Wishaw and was re-registered as RIL 9654. First Stop Travel acquired it in July 2003, and it was seen heading along Mosspark Boulevard on the 134 service. It returned to McKindless for spares in May 2006, and was cannibalised.

MPL 123W was a Leyland Leopard PSU3E/4R/Duple Dominant II C49F, purchased new by London Country as their no. DL3 in July 1981. On disposal it joined Barrie's of Balloch briefly before passing to South Yorkshire PTE as their no. 93. It then worked for Isle Coaches, then Andy James of Malmesbury before export to Eire, where it became 81-KK-398 with Digan Coaches of Knockraha.

This Talbot Pullman was new to Kentish Bus as their no. 993 and came to Scotland to join the fleet of Argyll Bus & Coach of Wemyss Bay in 1996. Firststop bought four of them from Argyll, but they were pretty unreliable and didn't last very long. This one is seen in Jamaica Street in Glasgow city centre, while bound for Penilee on service 281.

H357 WWX was a Leyland Lynx LX2R B49F, new as Yorkshire Woollen no. 357 in July 1991. It passed to Arriva Yorkshire with the business before sale to South Gloucestershire Bus & Coach. It passed to City Sprinter in 2007, and was photographed passing through Shawlands.

YE52 FHH is an Optare Solo M850 B28F, purchased new by Richmond of Epsom as their OP1 in November 2002. It is now with Avondale and was captured in Clydebank. The Solo is an integral midibus built in a modular design, with steel frame and GRP panels. It is powered by a Mercedes-Benz OM904LA engine, which produces 122 bhp or 147 bhp according to specification, and it is typically mated to an Allison 2000 automatic gearbox.

SF04 RHU was a Transbus Dart SLF B37F, delivered new to McColl's of Balloch in April 2004. The registration plate was very apt as the service it was intended for served the village of Rhu. The bus was supplied at a generous discount as there was no warranty included, because on 31 March 2004 TransBus International was put into administration. The bus later passed to Nu-Venture for further service.

PJJ 349S was a Leyland National 10351A/1R B41F, new as East Kent no. 1349 in October 1977. It passed to Crainey's of Kilsyth in 1989 and was seen working on the C41 service, which ran in competition with the similar Kelvin Scottish route 41, linking Cumbernauld to Kilsyth.

D521 DSX was a Leyland Tiger TRBTL11/2RH/Alexander P Type B57F, new to Fife Scottish as their fleet number FLT21 in March 1987. It then joined John Walker's Scotway fleet. After the demise of Scotway it passed to Dart Buses of Paisley. The livery is almost a combination of Barbie and Arriva. The bus was caught in Glasgow city centre while running on service 3 to Barrhead.

J397 GKH was a Dennis Dart 8.5SDL/Plaxton Pointer B28F new as London Buses no. DR97 in March 1992. It passed to the privatised Metroline company in November 1994. On disposal in September 2003 it was acquired by Dickson's of Erskine for use on their Paisley to Glasgow route 38, but moved to A&P Coaches, t/a Local Link of Barrhead, in May 2008.

G195 PAO was a Mercedes-Benz 709D/Alexander Sprint DP25F new to Magicbus as their no. 306 in May 1990. It later moved to Bluebird Buses and on disposal passed to DJ International before reaching Skyline. It was caught leaving Silverburn Shopping Centre on the 25A service to Govan.

KX08 HMO was a MAN 12.240/Plaxton Centro B38F purchased new by Puma Coaches in April 2008, and is seen here as it passes Elder Park in Govan. It later ran for Colchri Coaches after the two businesses were merged. The Centro was launched on the VDL SB120 in February 2006, but was made available on the MAN 12.240 in 2007. It was discontinued in favour of the ADL Enviro300.

J512 FPS was a Dennis Dart 9.8SDL/Alexander Dash B41F, new as Bluebird Buses no. 512 in February 1992. It passed to Colchri and was given this unusual version of the livery. It was running on the Silverburn to Braehead service, which is still operated.

SK07 HMG was an ADL Enviro 200 B29F, delivered new to Glasgow Citybus in August 2007 and seen in Chalmers Street in Clydebank while working on the 84 service, bound for Gartnavel Hospital. The bus was later transferred to the parent West Coast Motors fleet and carries the fleet number 10721.

J627 KCU was a Dennis Dart/Wright Handybus B40F purchased new by Go Ahead Northern as their fleet number 8027 in February 1992. On disposal it passed to South Lancs Travel before reaching City Sprinter and was crossing Jamaica Bridge.

537 JTC was an Albion Nimbus NS3/Willowbrook B31F built as a demonstrator for Albion Motors, Scotstoun, in May 1959. It passed to Barrie's, and is seen loading for a departure on the Balloch to Balmaha service. It would later pass to Booth & Fisher of Halfway for further service.

OVV 517R was a Leyland National 11351A/1R B49F purchased new by United Counties as their no. 517 in September 1976. It sported a Mark II front panel after UC moved the radiator to the front end. John Morrow acquired it and it was snapped in West George Street in Glasgow. It passed with the services to Kelvin Central Buses in 1992 as their fleet number 1112.

N128 XEG was a MAN 11.220/Marshall B38F, purchased new by R&I Tours of London as their fleet number MM261 in April 1996. In June 1996 the company was taken over by MTL London, and in August 1998 this became part of Metroline. On disposal in September 2003 the bus was sold to dealer Fleetlink of Liverpool, and passed to Caledonia, Glasgow, one month later.

PGE 348P was a Daimler Fleetline CRL6-30/ Alexander AL Type H43/31F, delivered new to Graham's of Paisley as their no. D17 in July 1976, seen at the Govan terminus of the route from Linwood. The bus would pass to Park's of Hamilton in 1982 and then Athelstan of Malmesbury two years later.

P476 JEG was a MAN 11.220/Marshall B38F, delivered new to MTL London Northern as their no. MM276 in December 1996. It was acquired by Caledonia, Glasgow, in October 2003 and is shown on Jamaica Bridge in Glasgow wearing an advert for a local taxi firm.

L299 BGA was a Mercedes 709D/Eurocoach B24F that had started life with Dublin Bus as 94-D-2012 in 1994 as their fleet number ME12. It was one of a batch purchased by Avondale Coaches and imported into the UK. This one was sold to First Stop Travel, although all the rest entered service in Avondale's own fleet. It was captured in Govan bus station wearing the livery that all Walker Group companies would eventually adopt.

LPT 903P was a Leyland Leopard PSU3C/4R/Willowbook B55F, purchased new by Trimdon Motor Services in August 1975. On disposal it passed to Silcox of Pembroke Dock, then Thorne's of Bubwith, before joining Loch Lomond Coaches in 1988. It ran for around a year before being dispatched to Willowbrook for a new Warrior body. This view shows it in Dumbarton after being re-bodied. It later passed to Stevenson's of Uttoxeter.

HGD 875L was a Leyland Atlantean AN68/1R/Alexander AL Type H45/31F, purchased new by Glasgow (no. LA669) in April 1973. It was one of four purchased at auction by Duncan Stewart, to replace an ageing fleet of Bristol Lodekkas. It was turning in Prospecthill Road in the Toryglen area of Glasgow.

P240 OSF was a Mercedes 711D/Alexander (Belfast) B29F purchased new by Henderson's of Hamilton in March 1997. It wears the Henderson Citybus livery and was working on the 78 service linking the city to Kennishead. These new services used the M8 motorway and had hardly begun when Stagecoach launched a much larger network of new routes in the same area at better frequencies and using brand-new low-floor buses. Henderson quickly withdrew from the fight.

WDA 930T was a Leyland Fleetline FE30AGR/MCW H43/33F, new as West Midlands PTE no. 6930 in September 1978. On disposal it passed to McColl's Coaches, but had moved to Carlton Coaches by the time of this picture. It is seen in Clydebank on the short-lived Glasgow to Old Kilpatrick route.

S986 JGA was a Mercedes O810D/Alexander ALX100 B27F, purchased new by Henderson of Hamilton in August 1998. As can be seen, it carried an advert for Legs 'n' Co., a Glasgow lap-dancing club. The Mercedes Vario chassis was built between 1996 and 2013, and a total of 90,743 units were manufactured.

McColl's Coaches W494 OBX was a former Dublin Bus AV150, an Alexander ALX400-bodied Volvo B7TL. It was the first one to be repainted by McColl's and was captured in Balloch working on the 207 service. It had originally been registered as 00-D-70150.

K732 DAO was a Volvo B10M-55/Alexander PS Type B49F, purchased new by Cumberland Motor Services as their no. 732 in January 1993. It was damaged in the Carlisle floods and quickly disposed of to MacEwan's of Dumfries, later serving with the Clydebank Bus Co., DJ International and now Silver Fox. It is shown with DJ while working on their Glasgow to Largs service near St Enoch Square.

This Mercedes Benz 709D with TBP bodywork is loading in Glasgow's Jamaica Street on service 16 to South Nitshill in the south of the city. This covered part of the old Clydeside service 16, which was not surprising as the owners of Riverside were former Clydeside employees. Although this route was taken off, the company's buses were seen in the Paisley/Johnstone area until recently, but sadly the business collapsed in 2013.

R157 HHK was a Volvo Olympian-56/Northern Counties Palatine, purchased new by Stagecoach East London as their no. VN157 in May 1998. It was transferred to Stagecoach Fife as no. 16157 in April 2003 before disposal to McColl's Coaches, then to Pat Hynes for his PJ Travel fleet, and is seen at Dalmuir. It is seen awaiting collection by a dealer as it prepares to leave the fleet. It was a victim of spending cuts by Glasgow City Council, who have drastically cut back on school bus provision.

R986 SSA was a Volvo B10L/Alexander Ultra B40D, which had begun life as Dublin Bus VL4 97-D-59004 in 1997. It passed to McColl's and was rebuilt to single-door, and was passing through Clydebank on its way into Glasgow on service 204. It would later work for Tanat Valley as their no. 286. The Ultra was a Swedish body by Saffle, built under licence to Alexander in the UK.

17 CLT was an AEC Routemaster/Park Royal H36/28R, new as London Transport no. RM1017 in January 1962. On disposal in 1986 it passed to Strathtay Scottish as their no. SR4. Bellview Coaches purchased three of these Routemasters from Strathtay in 1992, with Dodge S56 D310 MHS travelling in the other direction. YTS 973A retained Perth City Transport livery in this view taken in Jamaica Street in Glasgow.

YPJ 207Y was a Leyland Tiger TRCTL11/3R/Plaxton C50F, new as Alder Valley no. 1207 in June 1983. It was acquired by Midland Red North and re-bodied by East Lancs with a sixty-one-seat EL2000 bus body in December 1991. It then passed to Arriva Midlands before purchase by John Morrow in 2003. It later passed to Abbey Coaches of Neilston for school contracts.

FFR 169S was a Bristol VRT/SL3/ECW CH70F, new to Burnley & Pendle (no. 169) in May 1978. It was purchased by Green's of Kirkintilloch in January 1991 and used on their service network. In December 1991 the services passed to Kelvin Central Buses. It ran until June 1993, when it was sold to Nottingham Omnibus. It only lasted a year there before being sold again, this time going to Happy Days of Woodseaves, who ran it until 1997 when it was scrapped.

FP51 AOJ was an Optare Solo M920 B30F new to Nottingham City Transport as their fleet number 131 in October 2001. On disposal it was purchased by Skyline Travel Services, and was working service 25 in North Pollok. This was the second incarnation of Skyline, under the ownership of Ann McKay.

XXI 1435 is a Leyland Tiger TR2R/Alexander (Belfast) B64F, new as Ulsterbus no. 1435 in September 1992. It was one of a large batch purchased by Marbill of Beith and up-seated. It joined Gibson's in 2014 to help cope with increased school contracts and was caught working on the ASDA contract near Summerston.

V316 DSL was a Dennis Dart SPD/East Lancs DP43F, purchased new by Strathtay as their no. 316 in November 1999. It became Stagecoach no. 33266 when they acquired the business. On disposal in 2011 it joined McColl's Coaches, and was seen passing through Clydebank. It was resold to Go Travel of Carluke and re-registered as L777 GOT before sale to WJC Coaches in 2013.

V171 EFS was a Dennis Dart SPD/Plaxton Pointer B42F, purchased new by Lothian as their no. 171 in February 2000. It was one of a pair that joined Citybus in 2009 to replace two Ikarus-bodied DAFs, and was emerging from the gloom of 'The Hielan'man's Umbrella' in Glasgow while working on service 17.

WBN 467T was a Leyland National 11351A/1R B49F new to Lancashire United (no. 548) in June 1979. On disposal it passed to Cambus, and was one of many purchased in bulk by Green's of Kirkintilloch and operated in service until it passed to Kelvin Central Buses with the routes in 1991. It was photographed on its way to its terminus at Renfrew Street in Glasgow.

L841 CDG was a Volvo B6-45/Alexander Dash B40F, new as Cheltenham & Gloucester no. 841 in June 1994. It passed to Caledonia Buses, and is seen on service 44 as it crosses Jamaica Bridge in Glasgow. On disposal it went to Mulley's of Ixworth, then Beaver Bus of Whetstone.

SN0 3LFV was a Transbus Dart SLF B29F, purchased new by Avondale Coaches of Clydebank in July 2003 for use on SPT dial-a-bus contracts. The Strathclyde Partnership for Transport (SPT) is a transport body responsible for planning and coordinating regional transport in the Strathclyde area of western Scotland.

OSJ 605R was a Leyland Leopard PSU3C/3R/Alexander Y Type B53F, purchased new by Western SMT as their no. L2605 in December 1976 and passed to Clydeside in June 1985. On disposal it would have a colourful career with Anderson's of Westerhope, Mike De Courcey, and Weir's Tours of Clydebank. As can be seen, it carried route branding for the firm's Braehead service.

M395 JGB is a Volvo Olympian/Alexander (Belfast) R Type, new to Dublin Bus as 95-D-236 (no. RA236) in 1995. It joined the McColl's fleet as their no. 3032, and was working a Dumbarton local service. On disposal in May 2012 it passed to Stuart's of Carluke for further service.

L740 PUA was an Optare MetroRider MR15 B31F, new as West Riding no. 740 in May 1994. It became part of Arriva Yorkshire before purchase by McGill's of Greenock in 2002. Colchri Coaches acquired it and repainted it in SPT livery, but the shade used was too dark. It was leaving Silverburn on the tendered 374 service, bound for Shawlands.

G350 GCK was the prototype Dennis Dart, which was fitted with a B39F Dartline built by Duple in August 1989. It is seen in Glasgow on demonstration to Green's of Kirkintilloch. It was decided to close Duple and the design was purchased by the Carlyle Group, who continued to build it.

SN11 BVC/D were a pair of Hybrid AD Enviro 200s delivered to Colchri Coaches of Renfrew in 2001, and were supplied with money from the government's green bus funding initiative. This rare shot captured them both together at Silverburn Shopping Centre in Glasgow.

H158 NON was a Dennis Dart 8.5SDL/Carlyle Dartline C25 B28F, purchased new by London Buses Ltd as their no. DT158 in January 1991. It passed to the privatised London United in November 1994. On disposal in December 1999, it was purchased by Russell Arden for his Glasgow Citybus operations. Citybus were taken over by West Coast Motors in January 2006 and this bus remained until April 2008, when it went for scrap. It was photographed as it turned into Argyle Street in Glasgow while carrying an overall advert for Endrick Finance.

P698 RWU was a Dennis Dart SLF/Plaxton Pointer B35F, purchased new by Armchair of Brentford in May 1997. On disposal in February 2003 it passed to Locallink of Bishops Stortford, but had moved to Davidson Busways of Bathgate by September. It then joined Dunn's of Cumbernauld and is seen on the local service.

SN08 AEM was an ADL Enviro 300 B60F built in August 2008 for Plaxton as a stock vehicle. It was picked up by SPT and allocated to various companies including Henderson Travel, Stuart's, Whitelaw's and, as seen here, Scottish Travel of Greenock. It was working on the X22 service from Greenock to Clydebank. It was later purchased outright by Stagecoach Western and allocated fleet number 27623.

YSX 927W was a Leyland National NL106L11/1R B44F new to Fife Scottish in 1980 as no. FPN27 and seen here in the village of Garelochhead on its way to Helensburgh. It later passed to Glyn Williams of Crosskeys. Weir's Tours, Mallard Coaches and the later Weirs-Mallard were all owned by Dennis Noble.

Y987 TGH was a Dennis Dart SLF/Plaxton Pointer B29F, purchased new by London Central as their LDP 187 in April 2001. It now resides in Clydebank with Avondale Coaches, and was caught passing through Clydebank on the 200 service bound for Linnvale.

J106 WSC was a Dennis Lance 11SDA/Alexander PS Type B39D, new as London Buses no. LA6 in May 1992. It passed to Stagecoach Selkent in September 1994, and was converted to single-doorway B47F in 1997. In January 1997 it was transferred to Stagecoach Ribble as their no. 186. By April 2001 it had been bought by Lancashire United (Bolton) and sold with the Bolton routes to Blue Bus. This firm was taken over by Arriva North West in July 2005, and the bus was sold to the Walker Group, Barrhead, in February 2007.

DYS 637T was a Leyland National 11351A/1R B52F, purchased new by McGill's of Barrhead in September 1978 and seen in Jamaica Street in Glasgow. It remained in service until October 1993, and was scrapped by the end of the year. McGill's specified full-width destination blinds as no route numbers were carried.

H153 MOB was a Dennis Dart/Carlyle Dartline B28F, new to London Buses (no. DT153) in November 1990. It passed to London United in November 1994. In February 2000 it passed to Allison's of Dunfermline and two months later became Stagecoach Fife no. 32343 when it purchased the business. On disposal in October 2003 it joined Birmingham Motor Traction and in turn was taken over by Flight's with the business. In January 2007 it joined Trustline of Hunston and was quickly resold to Tony Morrin of Glasgow for his Puma Coaches operation.

J619 KCU was a Dennis Dart 9.8SDL/Wright Handybus B40F, purchased new by Gateshead & District as their fleet number 8019 in February 1992. On disposal in 2001 it joined Glasgow Citybus, and was caught in Great Western Road. The advert on the side panels was a fashion at the time, and referred to as a '4 square'.

RSD 968R was a Seddon Pennine VII/Alexander Y Type C49F, new as Western SMT no. S2665 in June 1977. It became Clydeside Scottish no. 912 before sale to Midland Scottish as no. MSE29. On disposal Beaton's of Blantyre briefly operated it, then McColl's ran it on local services around Dumbarton.

H140 MOB was a Dennis Dart/Carlyle B28F, purchased new by London Buses in January 1990 as their no. DT140. It passed to privatised Metroline in October 1994. By August 2003 it was with Beta Buses of Alexandria, owned by Phil Docherty, although it would carry PD Travel fleet names.

H152 MOB was a Dennis Dart 8.5SDL/Carlyle B28F, new as London Buses no. DT152 in November 1990. On disposal in November 1999 it was bought by Russell Arden, t/a Glasgow Citybus, and ran until June 2004, when it was withdrawn and cannibalised for spares.

99-KE-11 was a Volvo B10BLE/Alexander ALX300 B40F, purchased new by Bus Eireann in 1999. It passed to Slaemuir Coaches of Greenock and was re-registered as T404 EGD. It was acquired by Canavan of Croy and is seen passing through Cumbernauld on the local service to Kilsyth.

F30 CWY was a Mercedes 811D/Optare StarRider B26F, purchased new by London Buses as their no. SR30 in January 1989. It passed to privatised London Central in October 1994. On disposal in 1998 it joined South Lancs, and by April 2000 it was a member of the Green Triangle fleet. John Walker purchased it from dealer Blythswood Motors in March 2001 and painted it into his LBC livery. This view shows it just out of the paintshops in Paisley before it entered service.

HXS 106H was a Daimler Fleetline CRG6LX/Alexander J Type H43/31F, purchased new by Graham's of Paisley as their fleet number D9 in January 1970. It was loading in Govan bus station for the return journey to Houston. It would remain in the fleet until 1981 before passing to Liddell's of Auchinleck for school contracts.

K581 MGT was a Dennis Dart 9SDL/Plaxton Pointer B32F, delivered new as London Buses no. DRL81 in July 1993. In April 2004 it was purchased by Avondale Coaches, and was pressed into service while still in London General livery. It is seen in Clydebank and would run for Avondale for five years before being sold for scrap in 2009.

CRS 60T was a Leyland Leopard PSU3E/4R/Alexander T Type C49F, purchased new by Alexander (Northern) as their no. NPE60 in March 1979. It passed to Stagecoach with the business and later passed to Colchri Coaches of Glasgow for further service on schools and contracts.

TSJ 79S was a Leyland Leopard PSU3D/4R/Alexander Y Type B53F, purchased new by Western SMT as their fleet number L2719 in January 1978. It passed to Weir's of Clydebank and was used on the service linking the town with Braehead Shopping Centre via the Clyde Tunnel. Note the route branding on the cove panels.

DBV 845W was a Leyland National 106L11/1R B44F, new to Ribble (no. 845) in April 1991. It was transferred to North Western, becoming their no. 301. K-Line of Leeds got it on disposal, and it later joined Russell Arden's Glasgow Citybus fleet. It was photographed in Glasgow, turning from Union Street into Argyle Street while working on service 17 from Duntocher. It would pass to Puma Coaches for use on school contracts.

NSJ 380R was a Leyland Fleetline FE30ALR/Alexander AL Type H43/31F, purchased new by AA members Dodd's of Troon in August 1976. Ironically, it lost its roof in a low bridge accident and was repaired using the roof from A1 Service OAG 757L. On disposal in May 1992 it passed to Alex Pringle, t/a Discovering Glasgow Tours, and was converted to open-top layout.

A833 SUL was an all-Leyland Titan TNLXB2RR H44/24D, delivered new as London Transport T833 in September 1983. It became a member of Stagecoach East London in September 1994, before transfer to Stagecoach A1 Service as no. 948 in January 1995. It passed to the main Western fleet in 1997 before sale to McColl's Coaches in August 2001, and is seen in Dumbarton.

BGM 96 was a Bristol Lodekka LD6G/ECW H60R, new as Central SMT no. B96 in February 1960. On disposal it operated on schools and contracts by Doig's Tours in the Glasgow area and was photographed on a football hire to Hampden Park in Glasgow.

LGE 724Y was a Volvo B58-56/Duple Dominant B55F, purchased new by Hutchison's of Overtown in November 1982. It was purchased by Graham's of Paisley in June 1987 and would become no. S3, later passing to McKenna's of Uddingston in April 1990 and Kelvin Central Buses as no. 1391 in March 1992, later no. SV401. It was withdrawn in 1997 and went for scrap to dealer Wigley of Carlton.

YJ06 LDV was a VDL SB120/Plaxton Centro B49F, purchased new by Glasgow Citybus in May 2006, seen turning into Argyle Street. It would later be transferred to Rothesay depot and carry the registration number J20 WCM. Glasgow Citybus was formed by Russell Arden in November 1999 and purchased by Craig of Campbeltown Ltd in 2006.

YD63 UYZ is an Optare Solo M960 B33F purchased new by Wilson's of Rhu in October 2013, and seen working a local service in Helensburgh. The firm began back in 1981 with two minibuses and business has grown considerably over the years. Fleet strength now consists of fourteen vehicles, operated from premises in Rhu.

W809 BGB was a Dennis Dart SLF/Plaxton Pointer B29F, purchased new by Canavan in June 2000. It was caught leaving Garthamlock terminus on route 38, introduced to compete with First Glasgow after an incursion by Firstbus in Cumbernauld. Eventually peace returned, with both operators retreating back into their own territories.

PO56 JFJ was a Dennis Dart SLF/East Lancs Esteem B24F, purchased new by Metrobus as their fleet number 233 in September 2006. It is now with Avondale and was heading through Partick when snapped. In 2008, Jamesstan Investments, an investment company controlled by the Darwen Group, purchased another bus manufacturer, Optare. Later, in June 2008, a reverse take-over was performed, with the Darwen name disappearing in favour of Optare's. Production of all the original East Lancs bodies ceased by 2011, and the premises in Blackburn closed in 2012.

J806 KHD was a DAF SB220/Ikarus Citybus DP44F, new to London Transport in January 1992 as no. DK6. It was one of a batch of ten used on Route 726 Expresslink. Route 726 had come under the control of London Transport after the collapse of the Green Line Network in the 1980s and was operated by its London Coaches Subsidiary. Unfortunately, they struggled to operate the route and it was passed on (with the vehicles) to Capital Logistics. On disposal in 2000 it passed to Russell Arden for his Glasgow Citybus fleet.

C806 KBT was a Leyland Cub CU435/ Optare B33F, new in June 1986 to WYPTE (no. 1806). It passed to Lofty's of Bridge Trafford before reaching Folley's of Clydebank and later went to Govan Minibus Co. It was loading at Clydebank Station on a circular service that linked Clydebank with Dalmuir and Duntocher.

P238 AAP was a Volvo B6LE-53/Wright B30F, purchased new by Speedlink Airport Services as their no. 238 in June 1997. It passed to McColl's in February 2010, and was passing through Clydebank on the 215 Glasgow service. The livery employed was a version of the old Duncan Stewart colours, and based on that of Viscount Coaches of Burnley.

There is little doubt that this shot was taken in Scotland, given the saltire flags on display coupled with the Scotrail livery carried on SK07 HMD. This little ADL Enviro connects the two mainline Glasgow stations with each other. Glasgow Citybus currently run this tendered service and proudly fly the flag for the Scottish independent bus operator.